GW01017672

A Way Through

Doubt

ELISABETH RUNDLE

Hunt & Thorpe

Lord, I see the winds of change
and I feel my faith sinking into my boots. Sometimes I
feel so confident and then the chilling mists of doubt
creep over me ... help me, Lord, convict my wavering
heart ... save me!
Save me from putting my trust in myself,
other peoples' opinions. Save me from putting special
emphasis on things, from
worshipping a person ...
Lord, save me!

Peter got down out of the boat and walked
on the water to Jesus. But when he saw the wind,
he was afraid, and, beginning to sink, he cried out,
"Lord, save me!" Immediately Jesus reached out his
hand and caught him. "You of little faith,"
he said, "Why did you doubt?"

MATTHEW 14:30, 31

Gideon asked:
*"If the LORD is with us,
why has all this happened to us?"*

Lord, I'm asking the same thing. The same timeless
question, Why? Help me Lord, not to waste time
wrestling for a reason when greater minds than mine
have found no answer ... why do I doubt? If I but look
back over my life I see the crossroads, I see the way in
which experiences and other lives have been woven
with mine, I see the guiding hand of the Lord over all.
Open my eyes, Lord, that I may feel your presence and
turn my doubting into trusting.

Faith is a gift – but the will has a great deal to do with it. Let me tell you this: faith comes and goes. It rises and falls like the tides of an invisible ocean. If it is presumptuous to think that faith will stay with you for ever, it is just as presumptuous to think that unbelief will.

FLANNERY O'CONNOR

As a mother in tender love watches her child so the compassionate Master watches his disciples. When their hearts are subdued, when in humility they pray for help, it is given them.

ELLEN G WHITE

You cannot prevent yourself from being assailed
by doubts. Sometimes they seem to come at you
from all sides. In fact there are three main
sources of doubt:

Doubts come from others around us; you
    certainly don't want what faith you have to be
    disrupted by the negative attitudes of others.

Doubts come from your own unbelief; the more
    you look at 'the mountain' the higher it seems
    and the more impossible to move.

Doubts come from Satan: no accusing thoughts
    come from the Holy Spirit, but from the one
    who wants to destroy faith.

COLIN URQUHART

O Jesus, in the darkness of night and grief
Thou didst utter words of surrender and trust to
God the Father. In gratitude and love I will say
with Thee, in my hours of fear and distress,
"My Father, I do not understand Thee,
but I trust Thee".

(Text of a plaque on a rock beneath one of
the ancient olive trees in the Garden of Gethsemane)

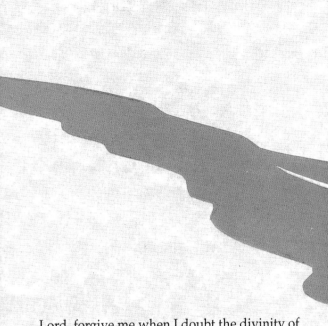

Lord, forgive me when I doubt the divinity of
Your Son, Jesus ... help me to realise how much
there is about Him that I do not understand; help
me to penetrate more deeply into the mystery of
His being and so learn more about You and
about myself.

MICHAEL HOLLINGS / ETTA GULLICK

No more we doubt Thee, glorious Prince of Life;
Life is nought without Thee, aid us in our strife;
Make us more than conquerors through Thy
            deathless love,
Bring us safe through Jordan to Thy home
            above.

EDMOND L BUDRY

I am so slow to recognise that everyone has passing flashes of doubt. Yet it is only in confronting my doubts, in being totally honest to myself, that I can work through to eliminate the emotions and fear which would undermine my faith. The darkest hour is just before the dawn – and dawn will come; the eternal law of night and day will not fail – neither will the Eternal Love which holds my life.

Lord,
I long to hold on to your promises:
all who come to You will find rest ... believing in you is
the door to a revitalised life ... all things are possible to
you ... You understand and know all things, even the
tiniest most insignificant sparrows are seen falling and
unsure.

Begone unbelief –
My Saviour is near!

Through all our trials we have a never-failing
Helper. He does not leave us alone to struggle
with temptation, to battle with evil, and finally
to be crushed with burdens and sorrows.
Though now He is hidden from mortal sight, the
ear of faith can hear His voice saying, "Fear not: I
am with you. I am he that lives and was dead;
and behold I live for evermore."

ELLEN G WHITE

*Though the mountains be shaken
and the hills removed,
yet my unfailing love for you will not be shaken,
nor my covenant of peace be removed, says the LORD,
who has compassion on you.*

ISAIAH 54:10

Jesus said to Thomas:
"Because you have seen me, you have believed;
blessed are those who have not seen and yet have
believed." Jesus did many other miraculous signs in
the presence of his disciples which are not recorded in
this book. But these are written that you may believe
that Jesus is the Christ, the Son of God,
and that by believing you may have life
in his name.

JOHN 20:29–31

My Lord, and my God.

Here in the maddening maze of things
When tossed by storm and flood,
To one fixed ground my spirit clings:
I know that God is good.

JOHN G WHITTIER

I believe in God, the Father Almighty,
Maker of Heaven and Earth,
And in Jesus Christ his only Son our Lord.

Jesus asked: "Who do you say I am?"
Simon Peter answered:
"You are the Christ, the Son of the living God".